For Swa,
the little hero
of tine & gert

Thanks to Dr.-Ing. Guy Van de gaer

First published in Belgium and Holland by Clavis Uitgeverij, Hasselt – Amsterdam, 2007
Copyright © 2007, Clavis Uitgeverij

English translation from the Dutch by Clavis Publishing Inc. New York
Copyright © 2015 for the English language edition: Clavis Publishing Inc. New York

Visit us on the web at www.clavisbooks.com

Firefighters and What They Do written and illustrated by Liesbet Slegers
Original title: *De brandweerman*
Translated from the Dutch by Clavis Publishing

ISBN 978-1-60537-232-7

This book was printed in June 2015 at Proost Industries NV,
Everdongenlaan 23, 2300 Turnhout, Belgium

First Edition
10 9 8 7 6 5 4 3 2 1

Firefighters
and What They Do

Liesbet Slegers

Clavis

NEW YORK

When there is a fire, there is danger.

Fires need to be put out very quickly.

Extinguishing fires is the work of the firefighters.

They come immediately when they are called.

"All units to the fire," says the dispatcher on the phone.

Firefighters wear special suits
that protect them from the fire.
On their helmets there is a shield they can push
over their faces and a lamp that will light up
when they walk into the thick, black smoke.
A neck flap protects them from falling sparks.

helmet

lamp

shield

neck flap

gloves

coat

pants

boots

walkie-talkie

The fire engine is ready and waiting.

Firefighters need a lot of things to extinguish a fire.

They use walkie-talkies to talk with the chief fire officer –

he tells them exactly what to do.

They connect the hose to the fire hydrant on the pavement.

They have a small axe and a beltline on their belts.

They will need those if there is something in their way.

hose

belt – axe – beltline

fire engine

fire hydrant

"We are on our way!" a firefighter answers in the fire station.
Quick, everyone!
The firefighters slide down the pole
because it's faster than taking the stairs.

The firefighters jump into their special suits.

They put on their pants, coat, strong boots, gloves,

and finally their helmets.

Don't forget the walkie-talkies.

"Come on, let's go!"

The sirens blare.

Everybody out of the way! Here comes the fire engine!

The chief fire officer drives in another car.

Will the firefighters get there in time to save the house?

The hydrant is on the pavement.

Working fast, the firemen connect the hose.

Now there will be enough water to put out the fire.

The chief fire officer talks into the walkie-talkie
and tells the firefighters exactly what to do.
A firefighter on the ladder sprays water on the roof.
Another firefighter sprays water from below.

Whew! The fire is extinguished and the house is saved.

The fire engine drives away quietly.

This time the sirens are off.

Look! A car can't drive because a tree has fallen
and is blocking the road.
"Just a minute, Ma'am," a firefighter says.
"We'll solve the problem."

Using the cable from the crane, the fire engine
tows the tree off the road.
"All set, Ma'am. Go ahead," the firefighter smiles.
"Thanks so much. You are a real hero!" The lady waves.

Help the firefighters!

A fire needs to be put out.

Which is the right hose?

Use your finger to follow the hose from the hydrant to the fire.